Quotes are from various authors and their names are at the end of the quotes.

Mama's Garden
A Poetic Coloring Book Journey
Original drawings by Bonnie McPhail

Printed in the United States of America all rights reserved under International Copyright Law. Contents and/or cover may not be reproduced in whole or in part without the express permission of the Author.

Dear Friends,

    Mama's Garden reminds of my childhood when I used to go pick flowers out of my mother's beautiful garden. Each drawing is original and designed to be on its own page so you can use a variety of coloring pencils, marker, pens or water color pencils, and there are beautiful life quotes across from each page to uplift and encourage.

Enjoy and God Bless!

From my heart to yours…

Bonnie McPhail

Mama's Garden

A Poetic Coloring Book Journey

By

Bonnie McPhail

Serenity

A Cup of coffee and the stillness of the moment.

A place of quiet surrender.

I listen...

I ponder...

I remember...

And then I learn.

Your Spirit whispers my name,

I am filled with the realization that the God of the universe

Loves me...

Perfect peace, perfect joy, and perfect purpose.

You are the one who gives beautiful gifts to open.

Unexpeceted.

Unearned.

Undeserved.

The knowing brings delight

"Stay patient and trust your journey."

Unknown

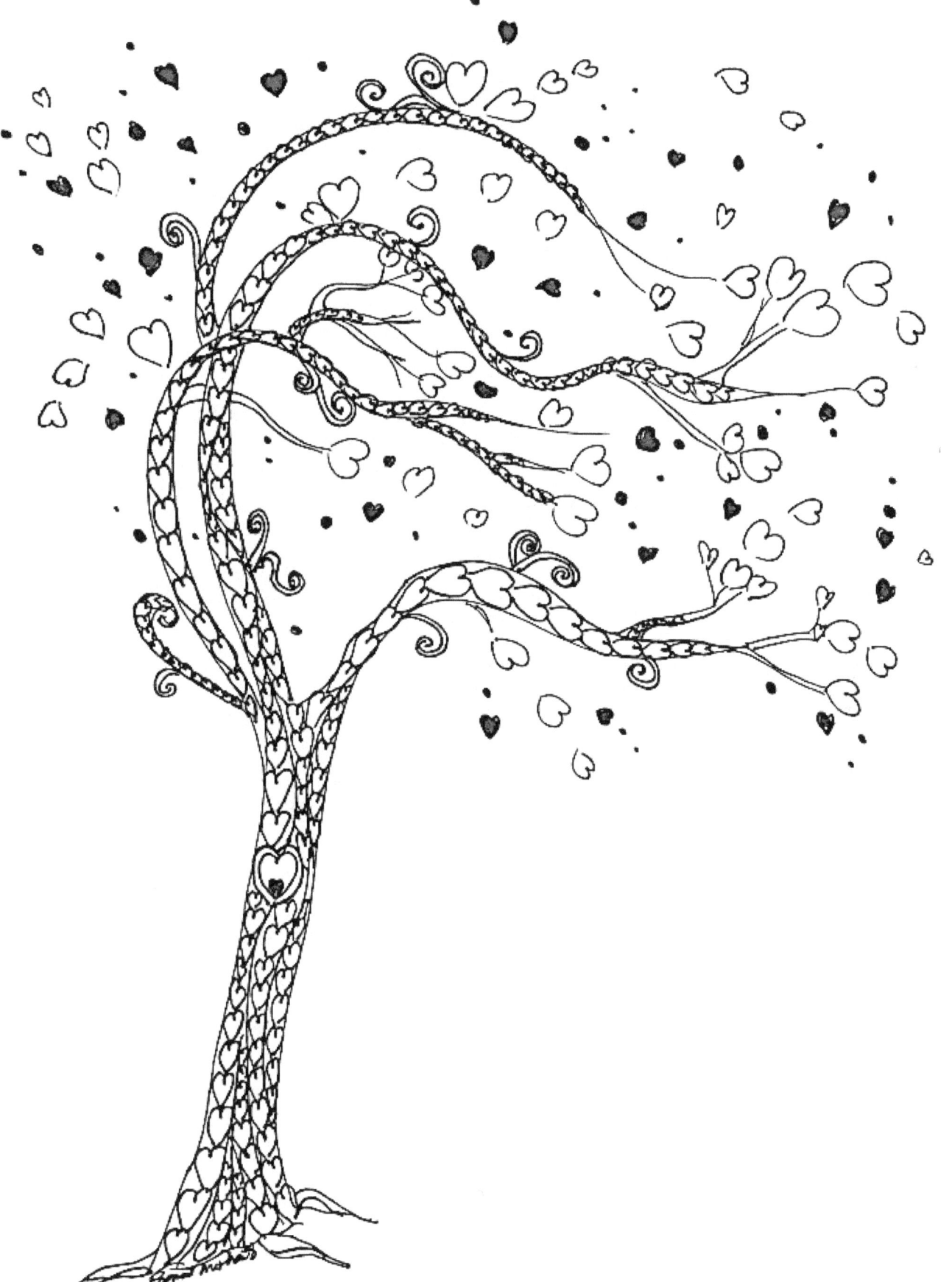

"The best is yet to come!"

Unknown

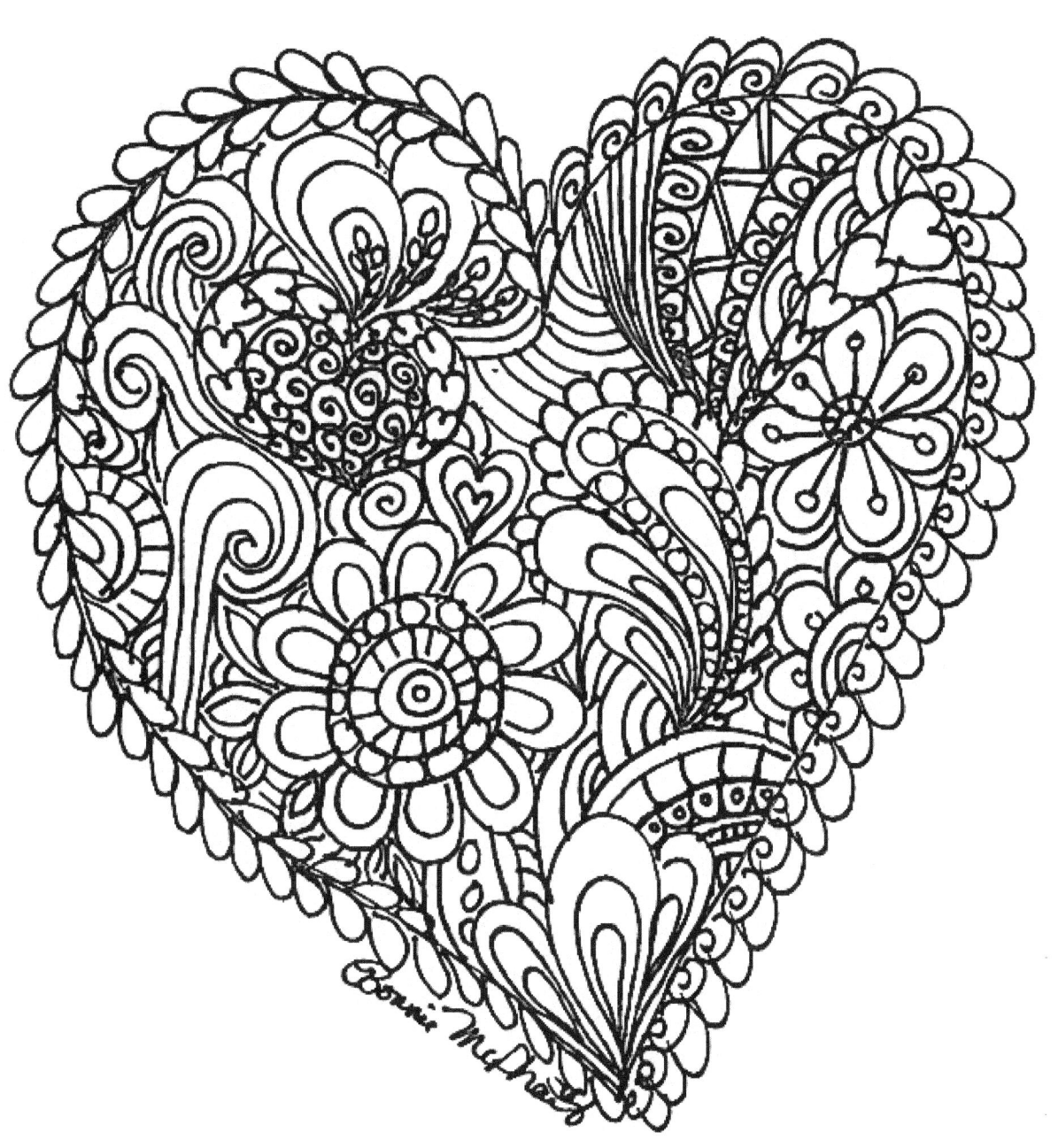

"Make your life a masterpiece; Imagine no limitations on what you can be, have, or do." Brian Tracy

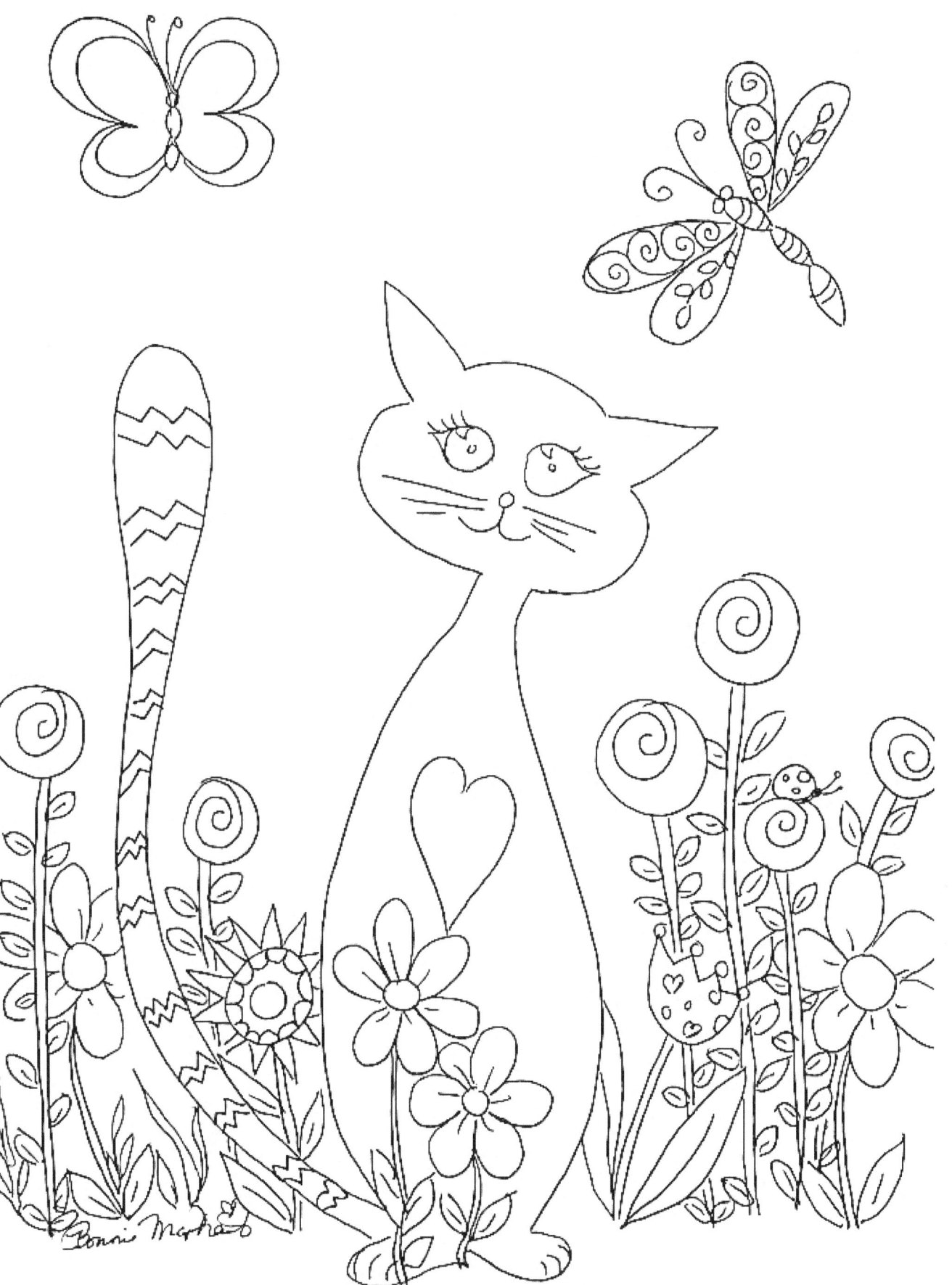

"The best and most beautiful things in the world

cannot be seen or touched

they must be felt with the heart."

Helen Keller

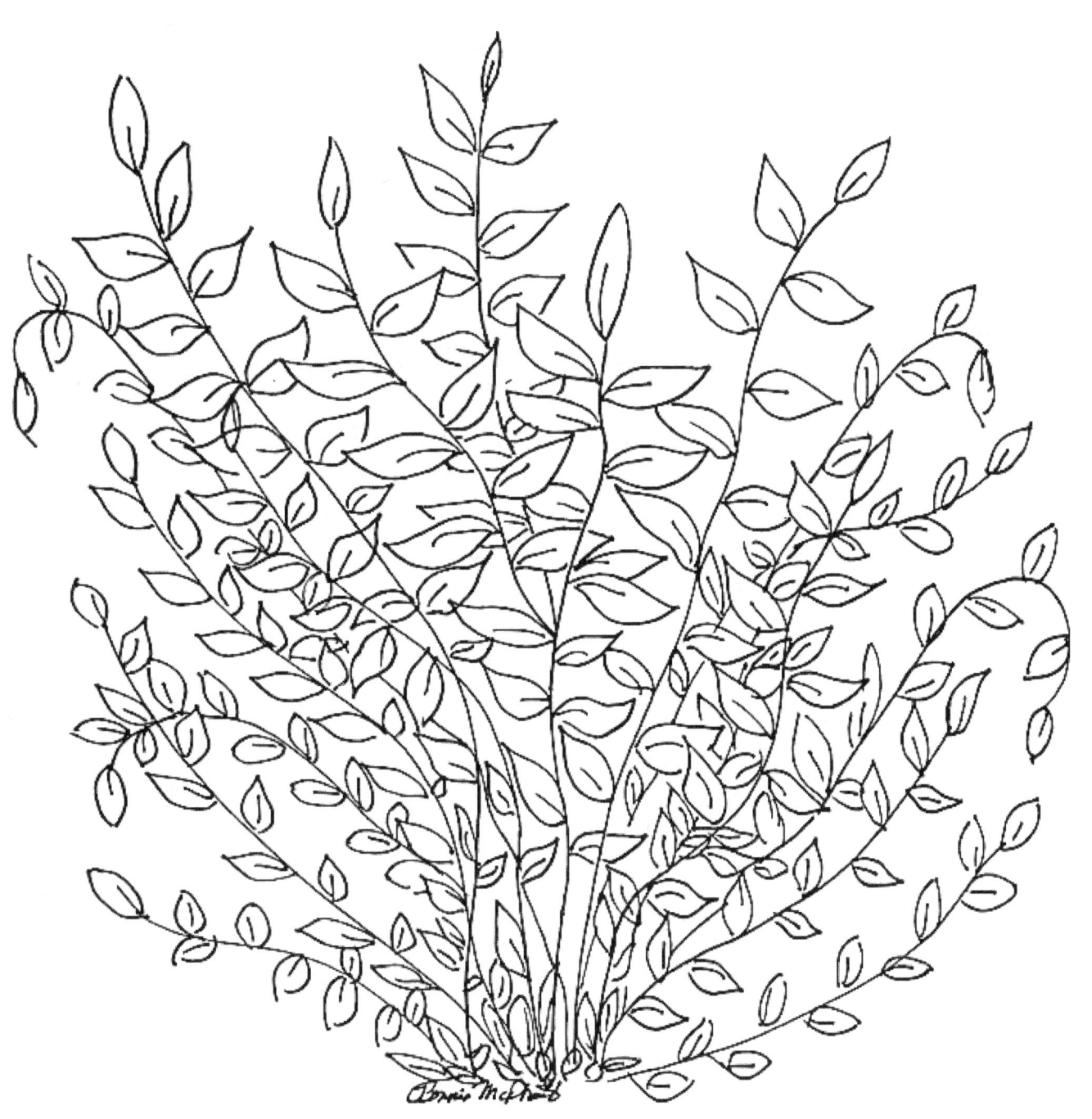

"Many people will walk in and out of your life, but only true friends will leave footprints."

Eleanor Roosevelt

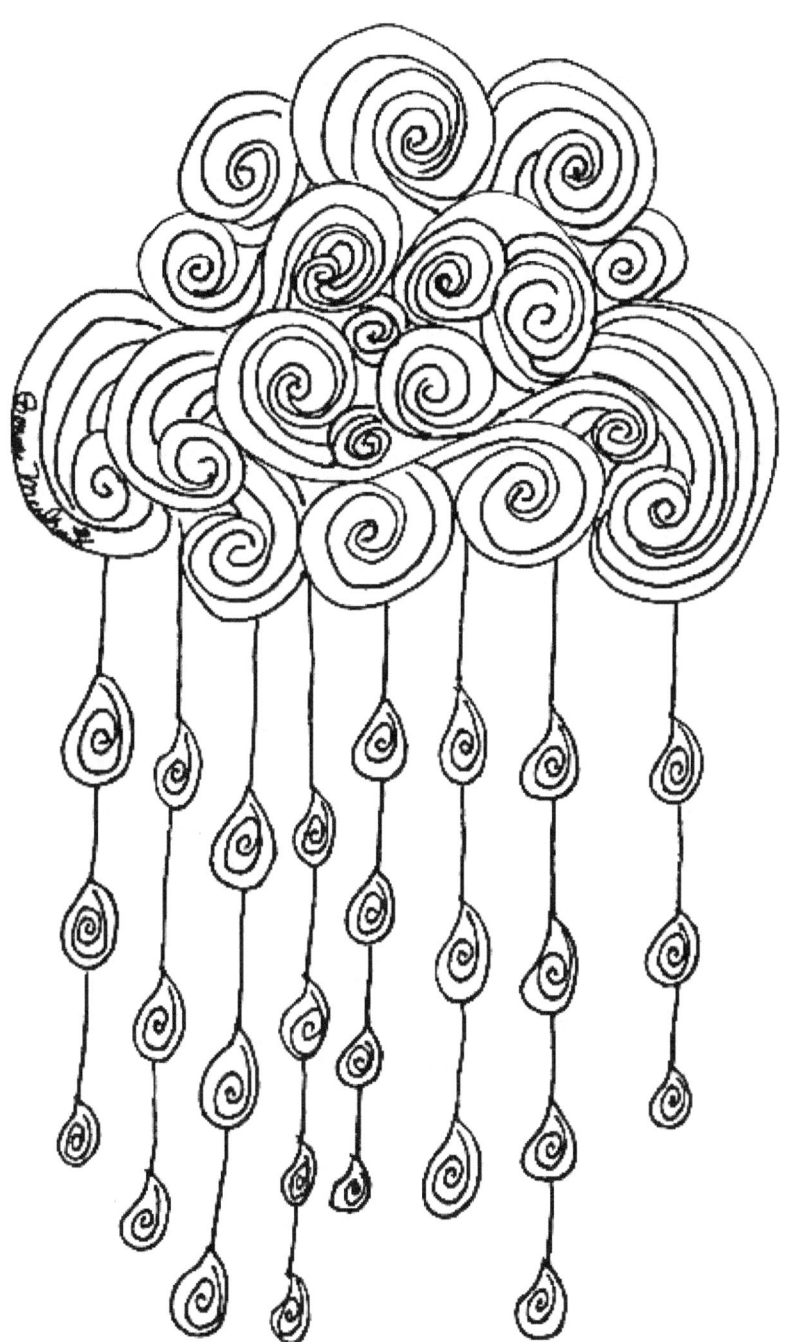

"Don't let yesterday take up too much of today."

Will Rogers

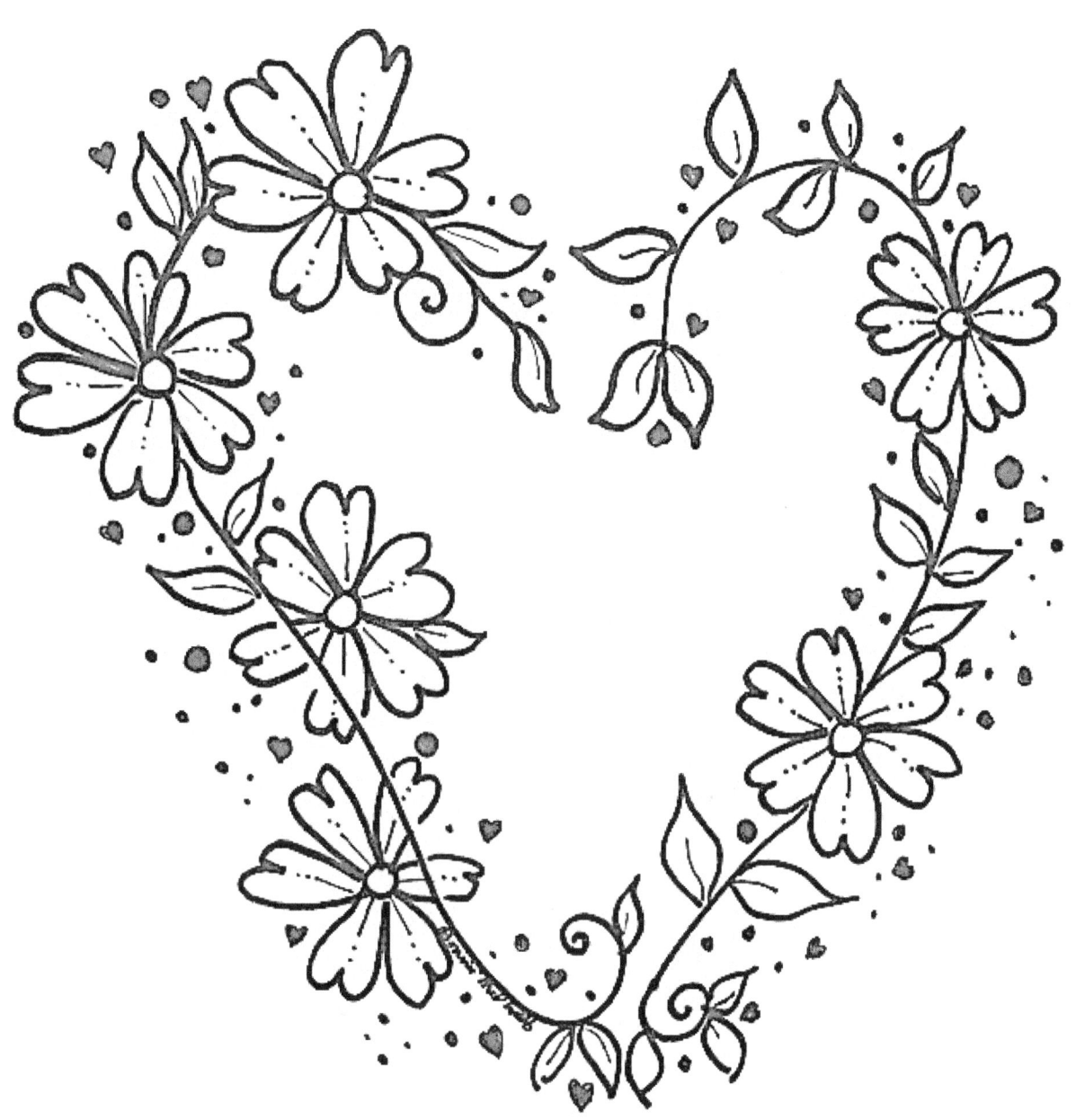

"You don't always need a plan.

Sometimes you just need to breathe,

trust,

let go,

and see what happens."

Mandy Hale

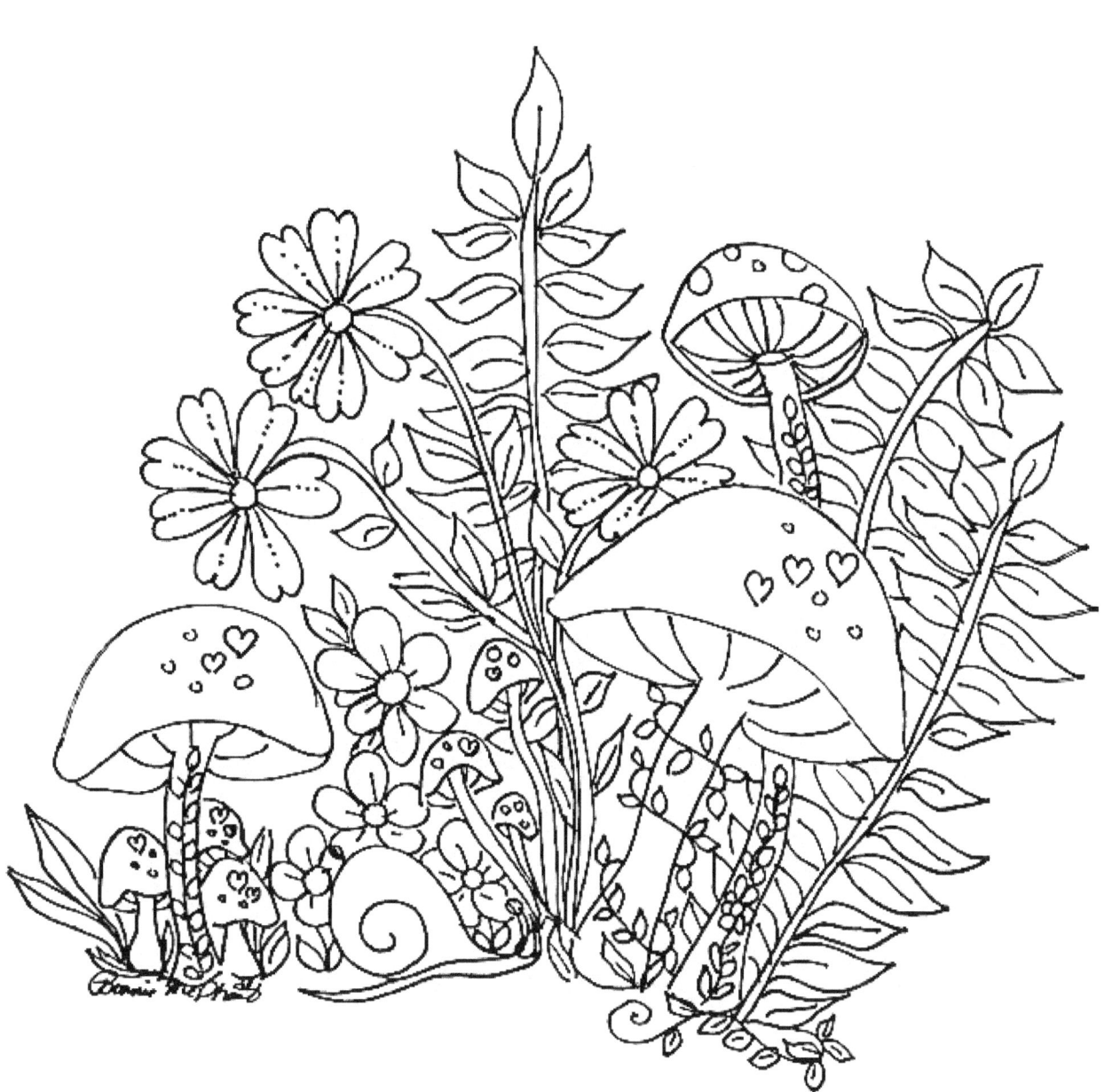

"Learn from yesterday.

Live for today.

Hope for tomorrow."

Albert Einstein

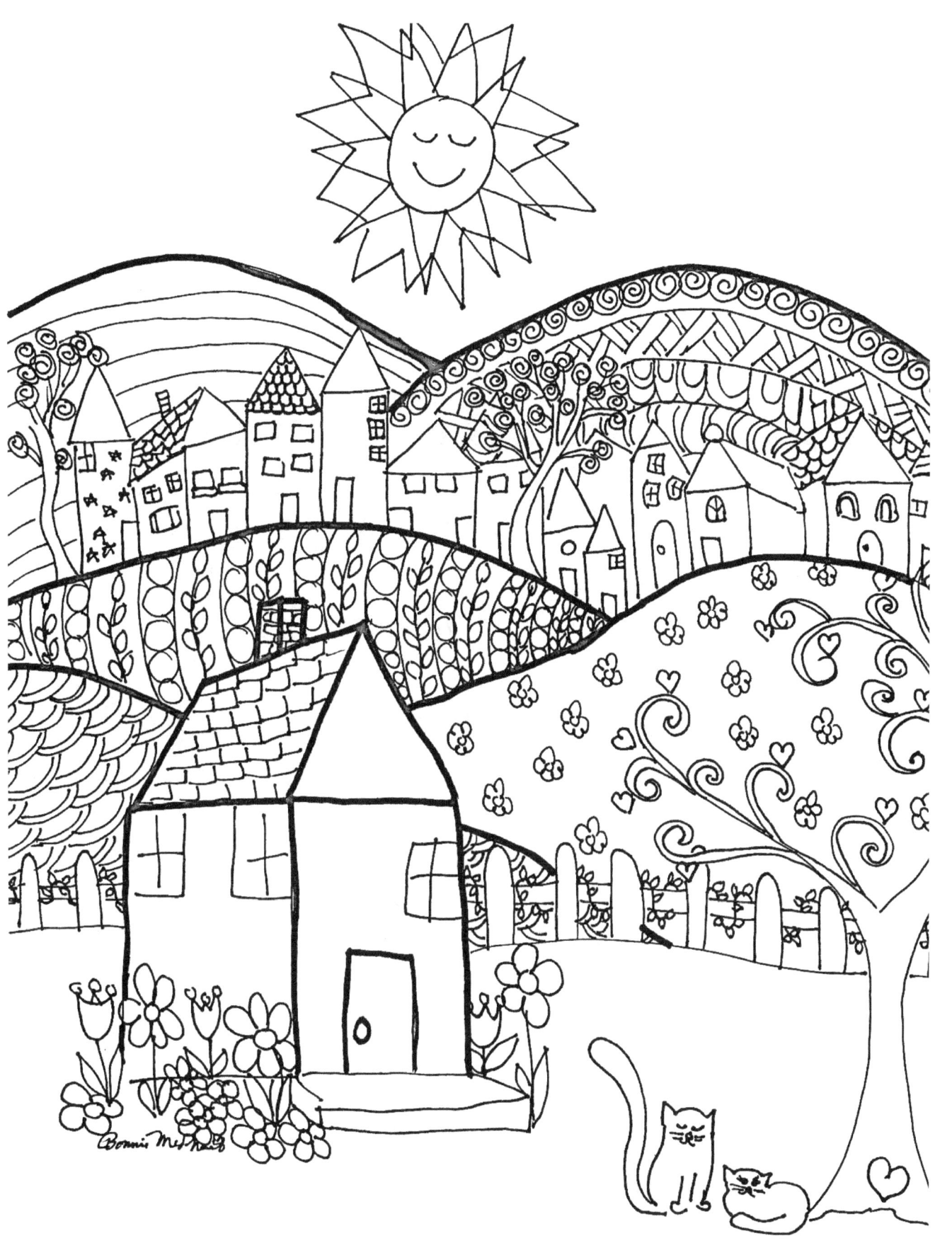

"Keep your face always towards the sunshine,

And shadows will fall behind you."

Walt Whitman

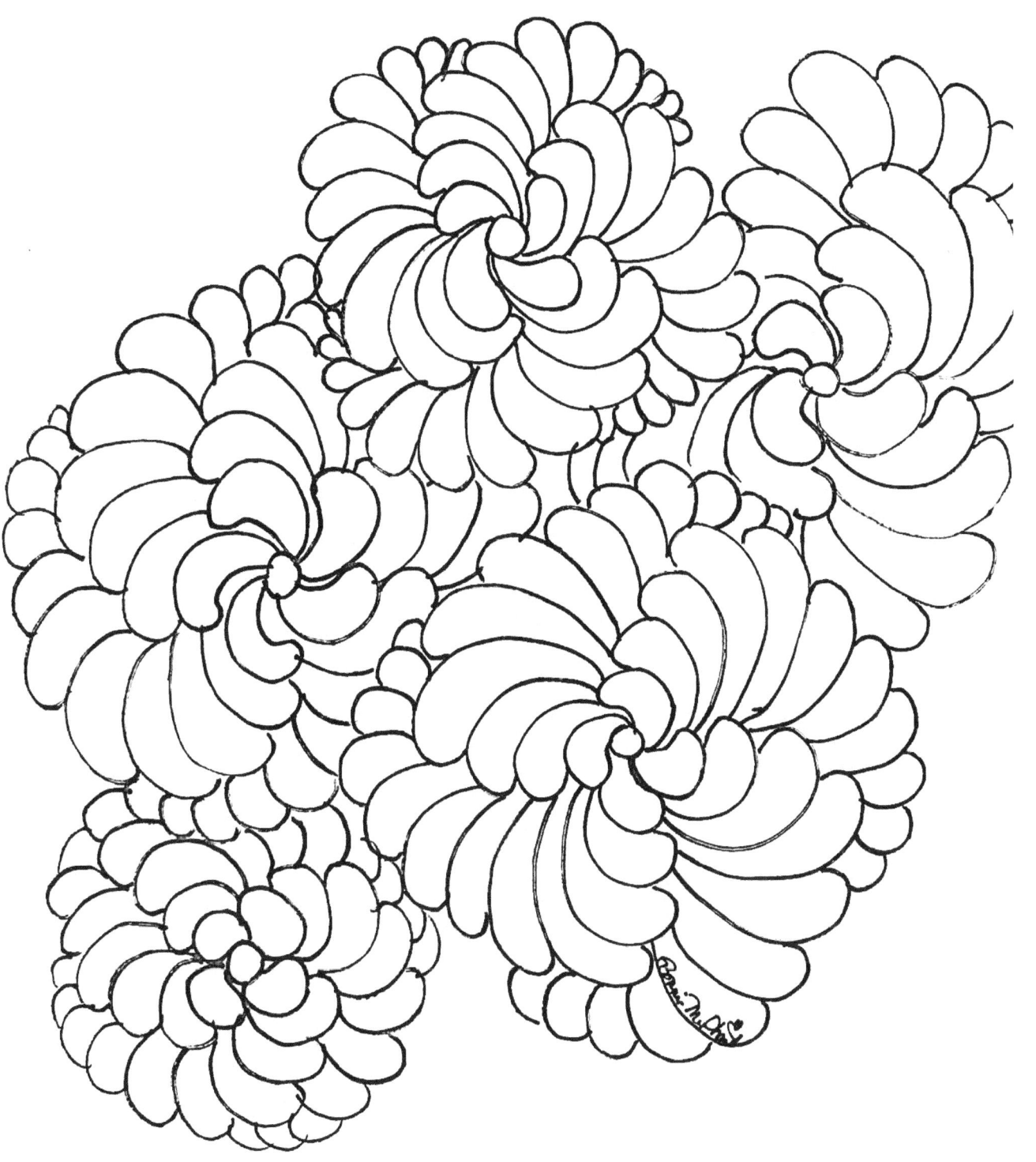

"Don't wait.

The time will never be just right."

Napoleon Hill

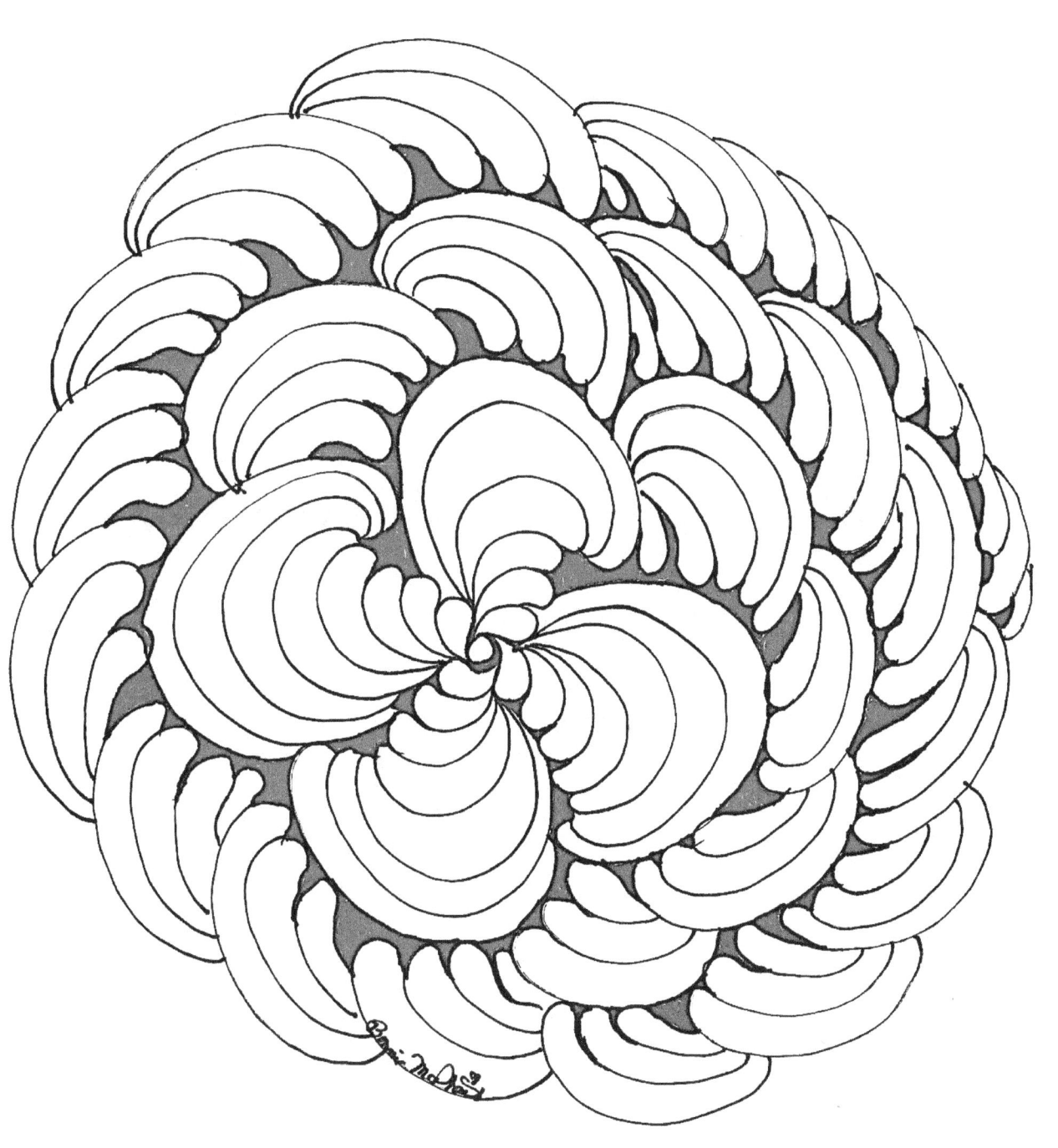

"When you can't find the sunshine,

Be the sunshine!"

Ed Lester

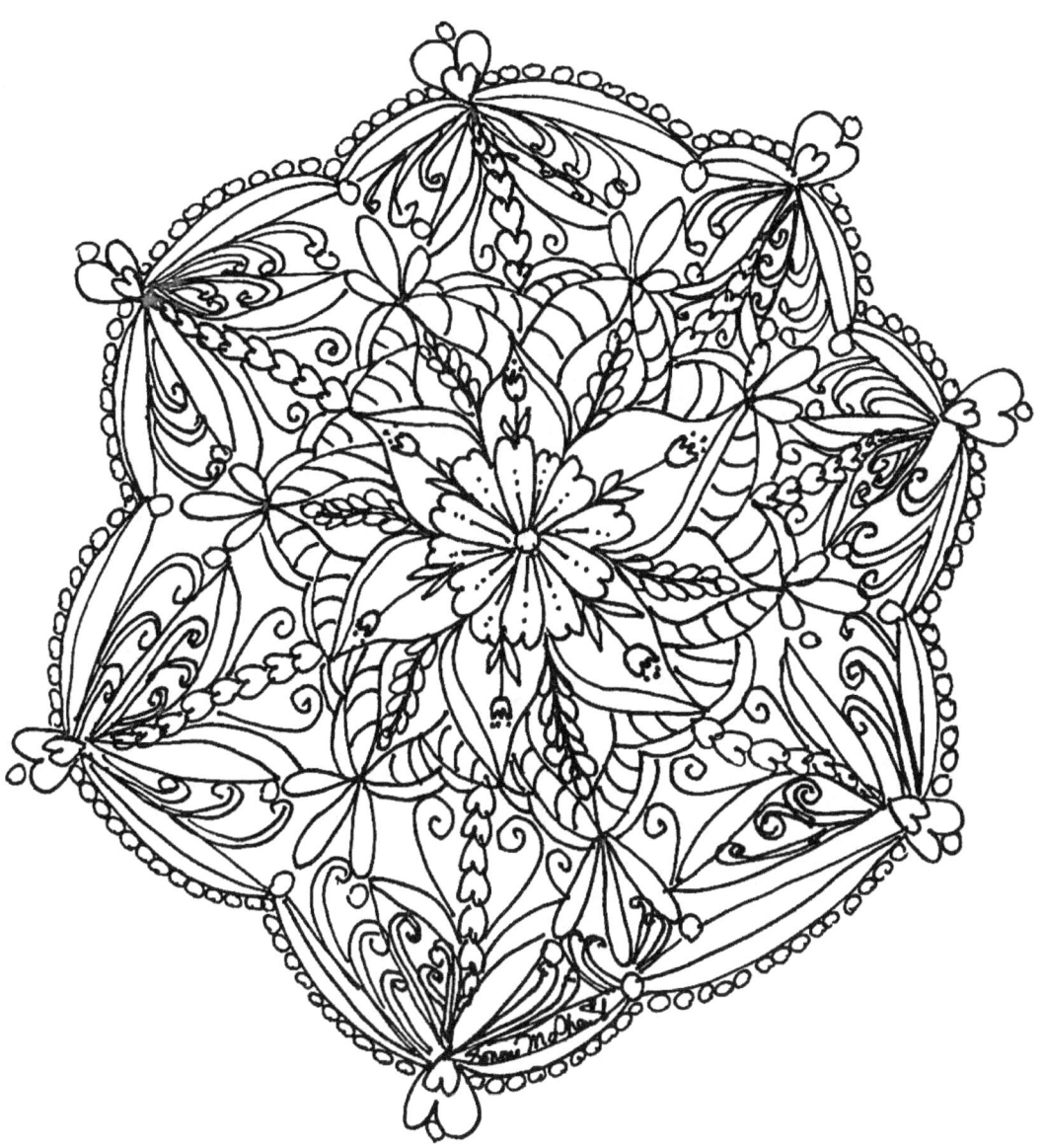

"Love the life you live.

Live the life you love."

Bob Marley

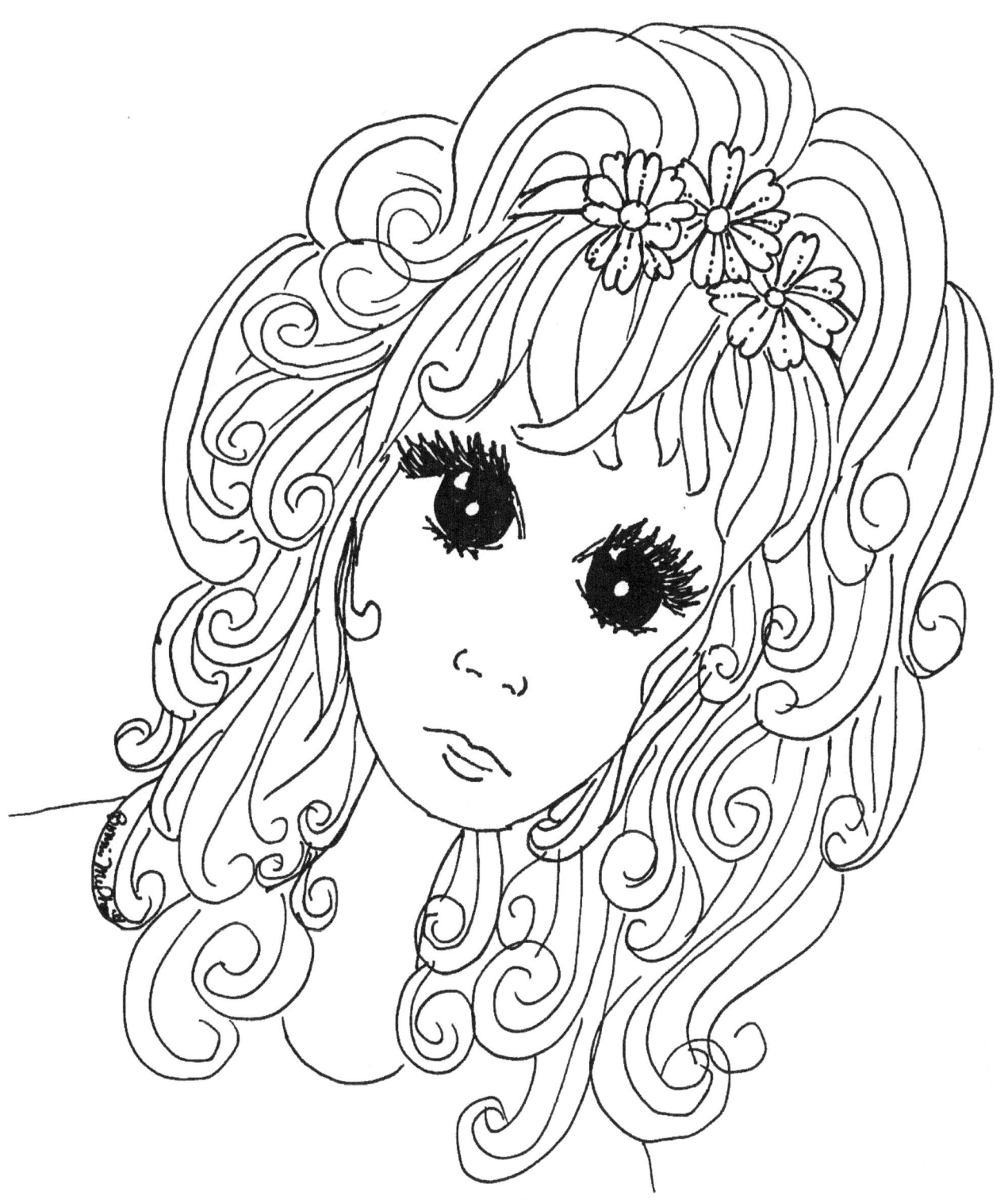

"Be the person who decided

To go for it!"

Unknown

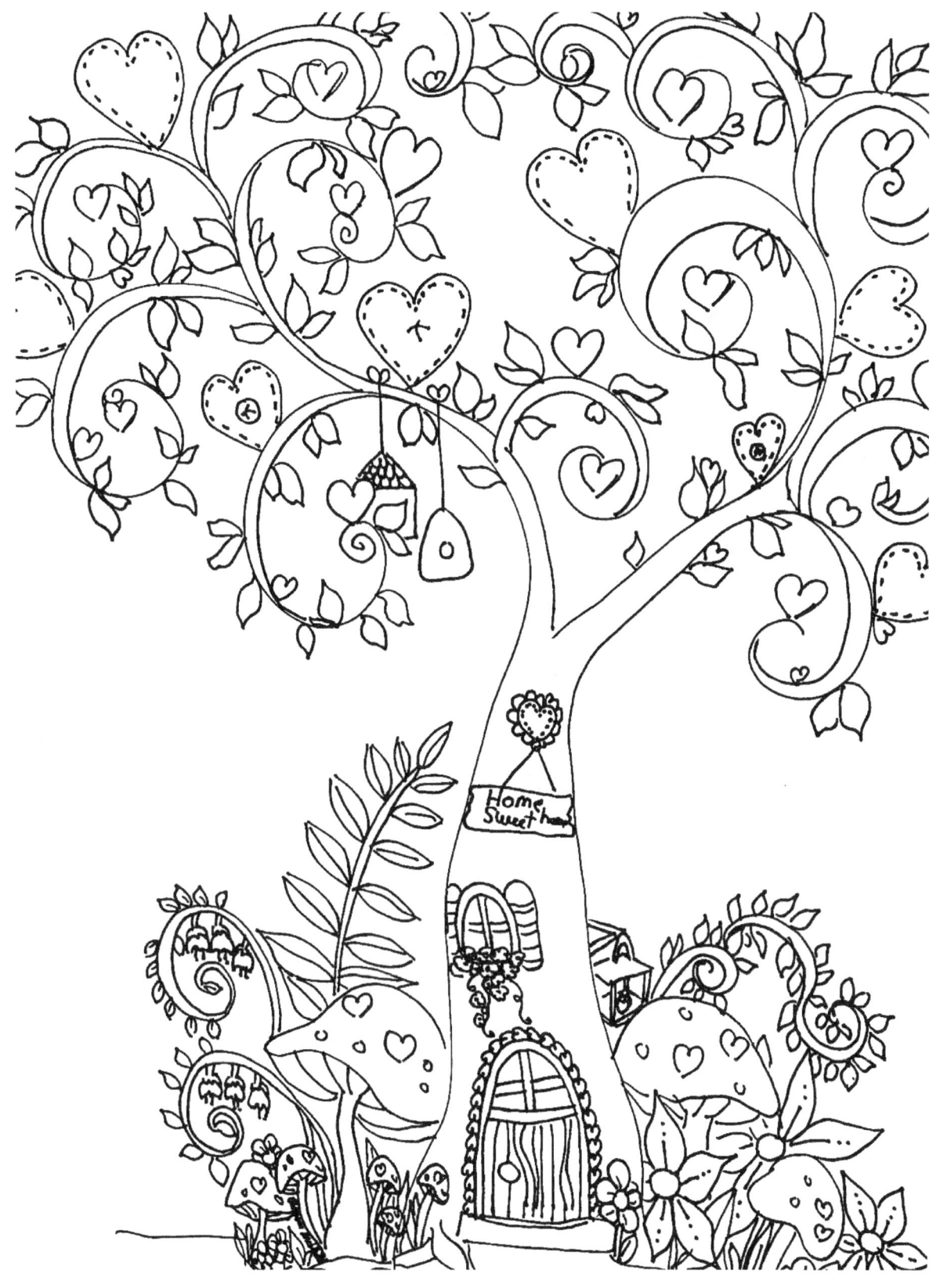

"Create the highest,

grandest vision possible for your life,

because you become what you believe."

Ed Lester

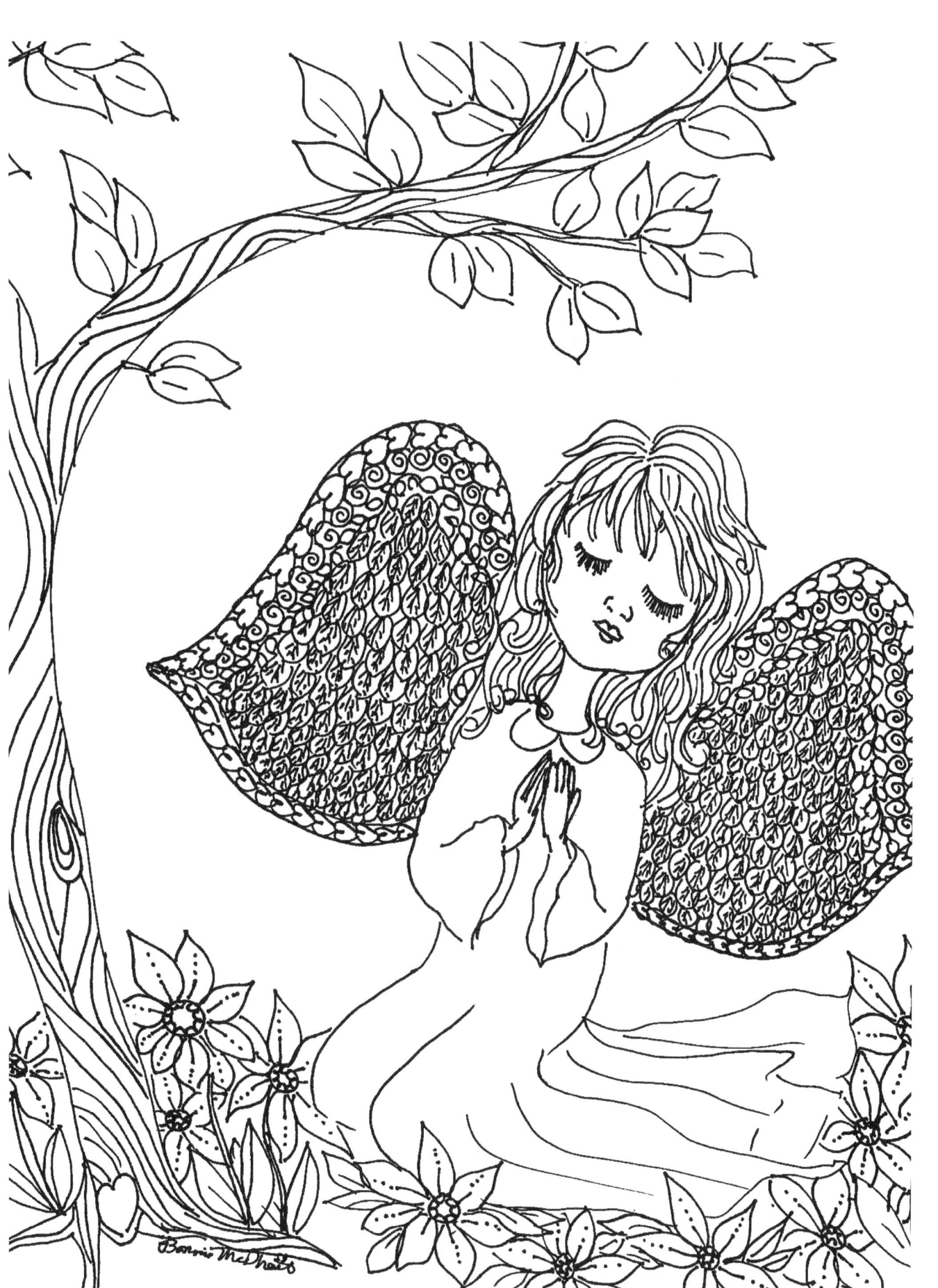

"With the new day comes new strength and new thoughts."

Eleanor Roosevelt

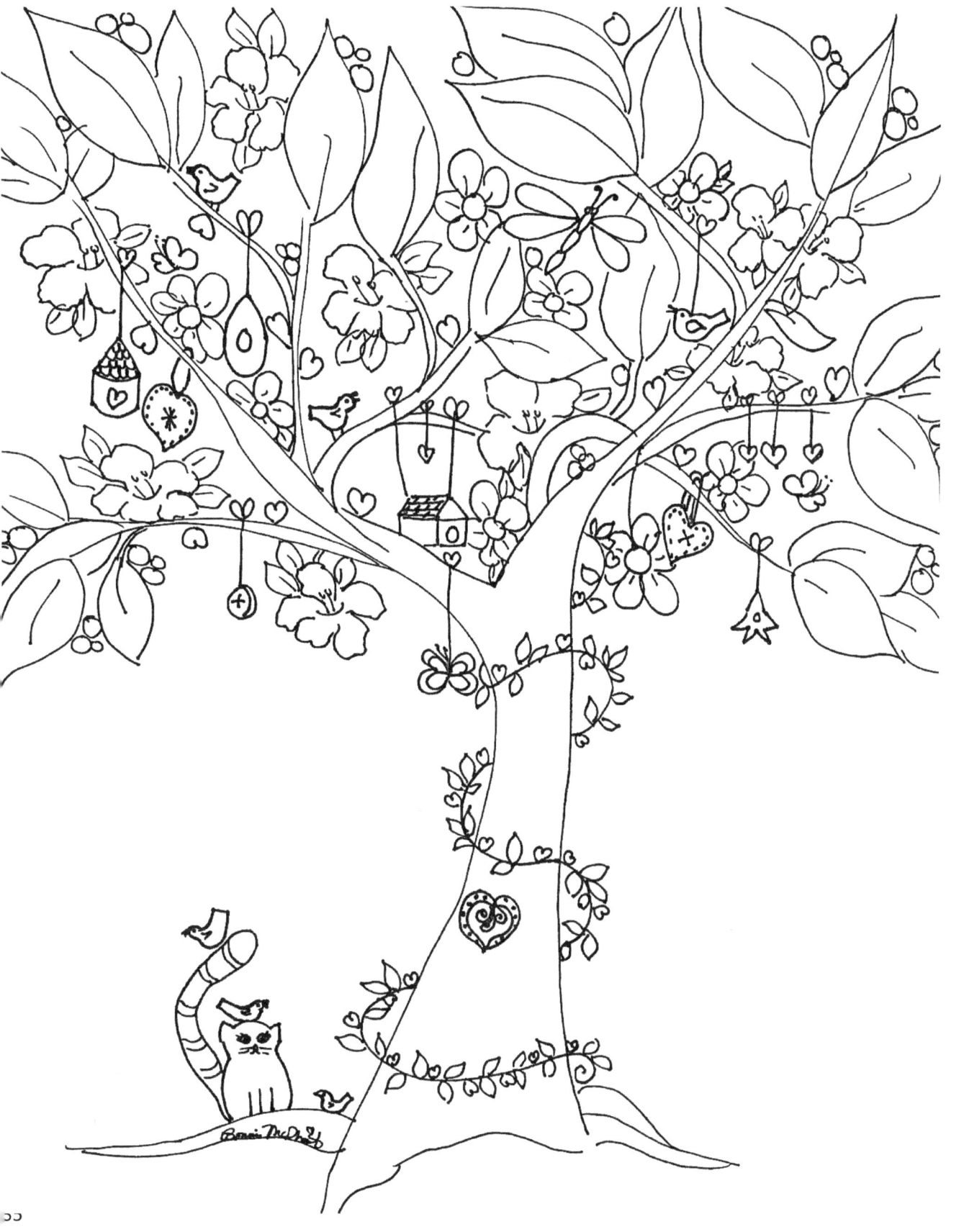

"Be strong not rude.

Be kind not weak.

Be proud not arrogant."

Worshipgifs.org

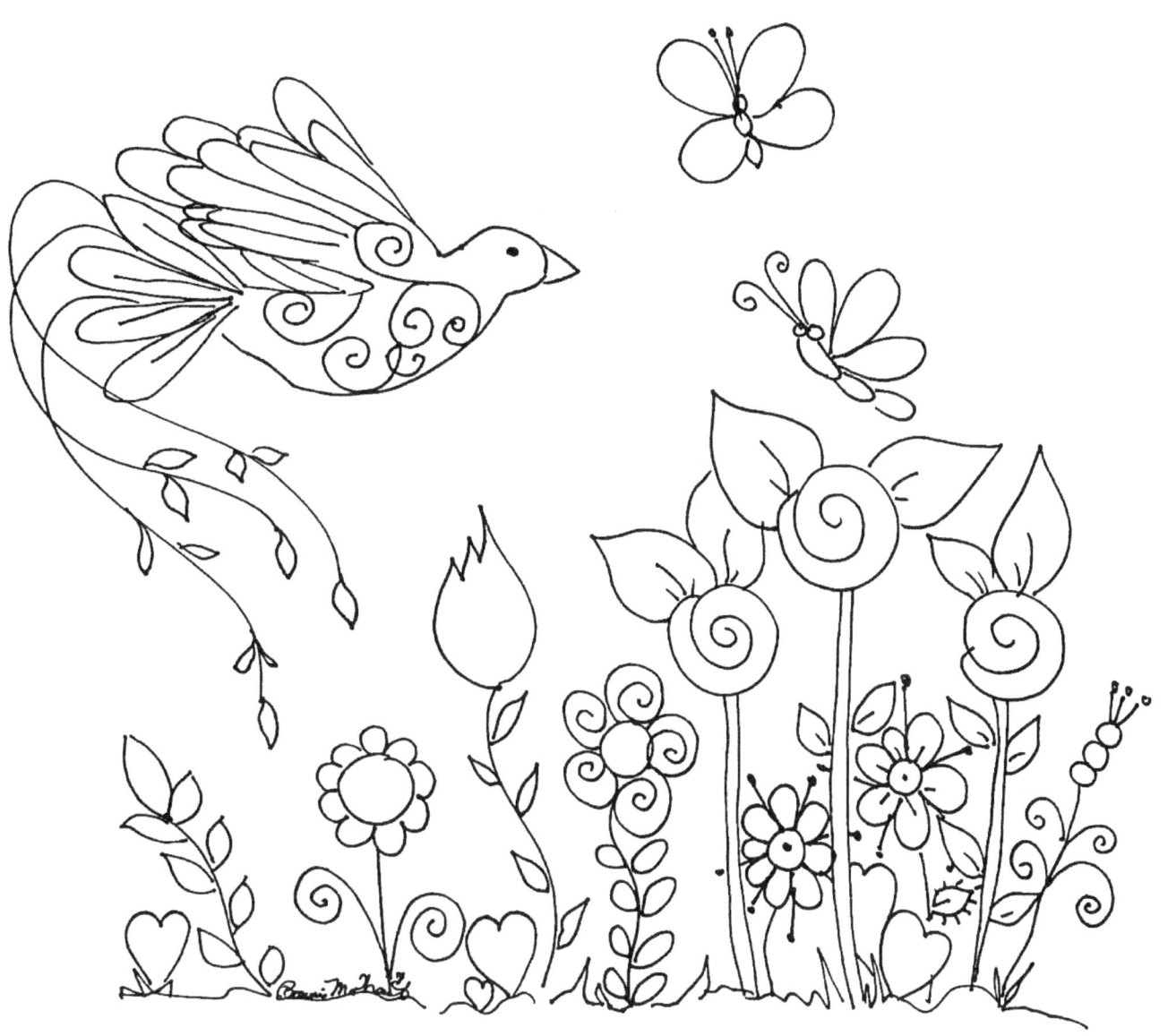

"Do something great!"

lifehack

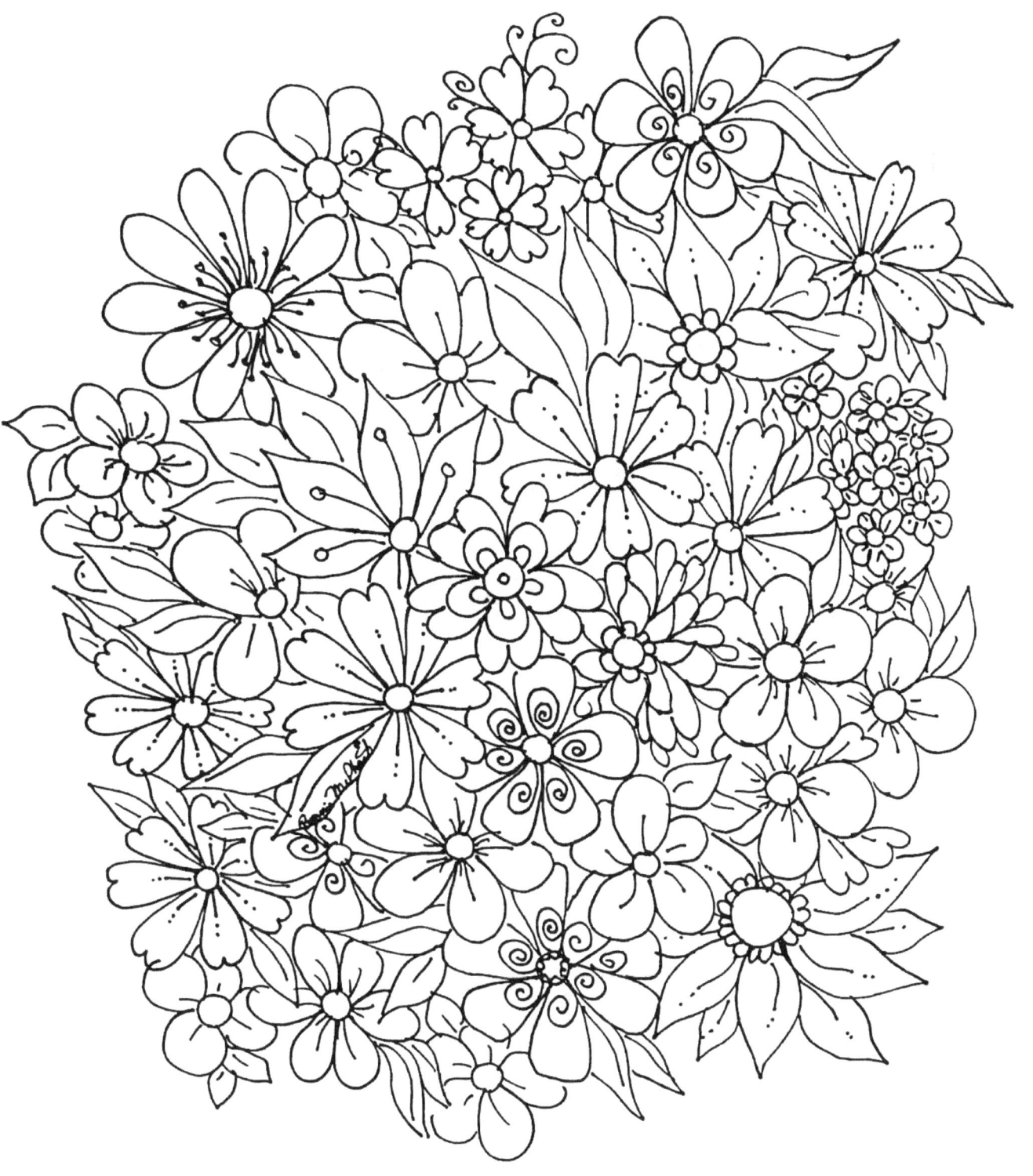

"Every day may not be good, but there is something good in every day."

Unknown

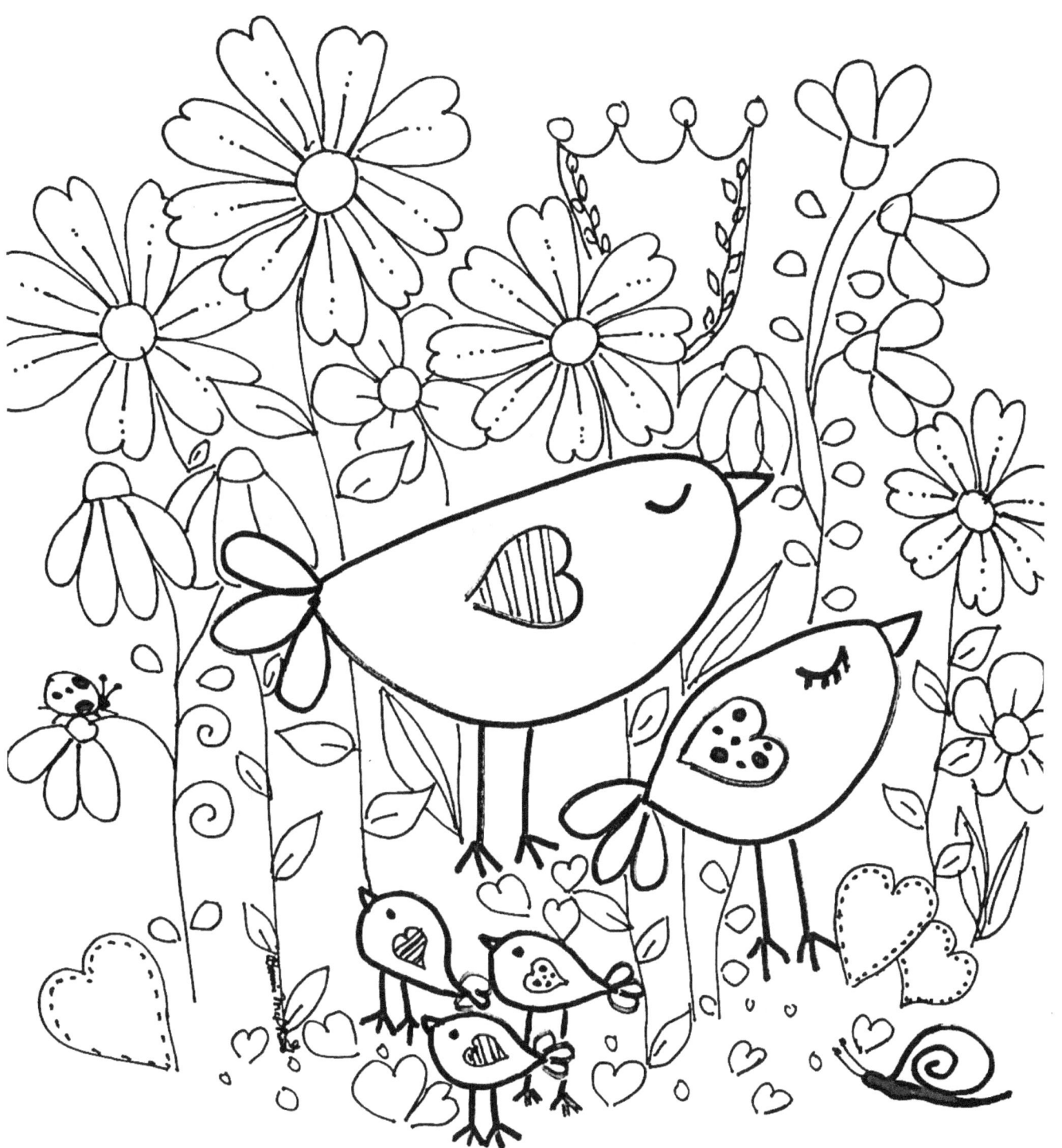

"Love is when the other person's happiness is more important than your own."

Lifehacks.io

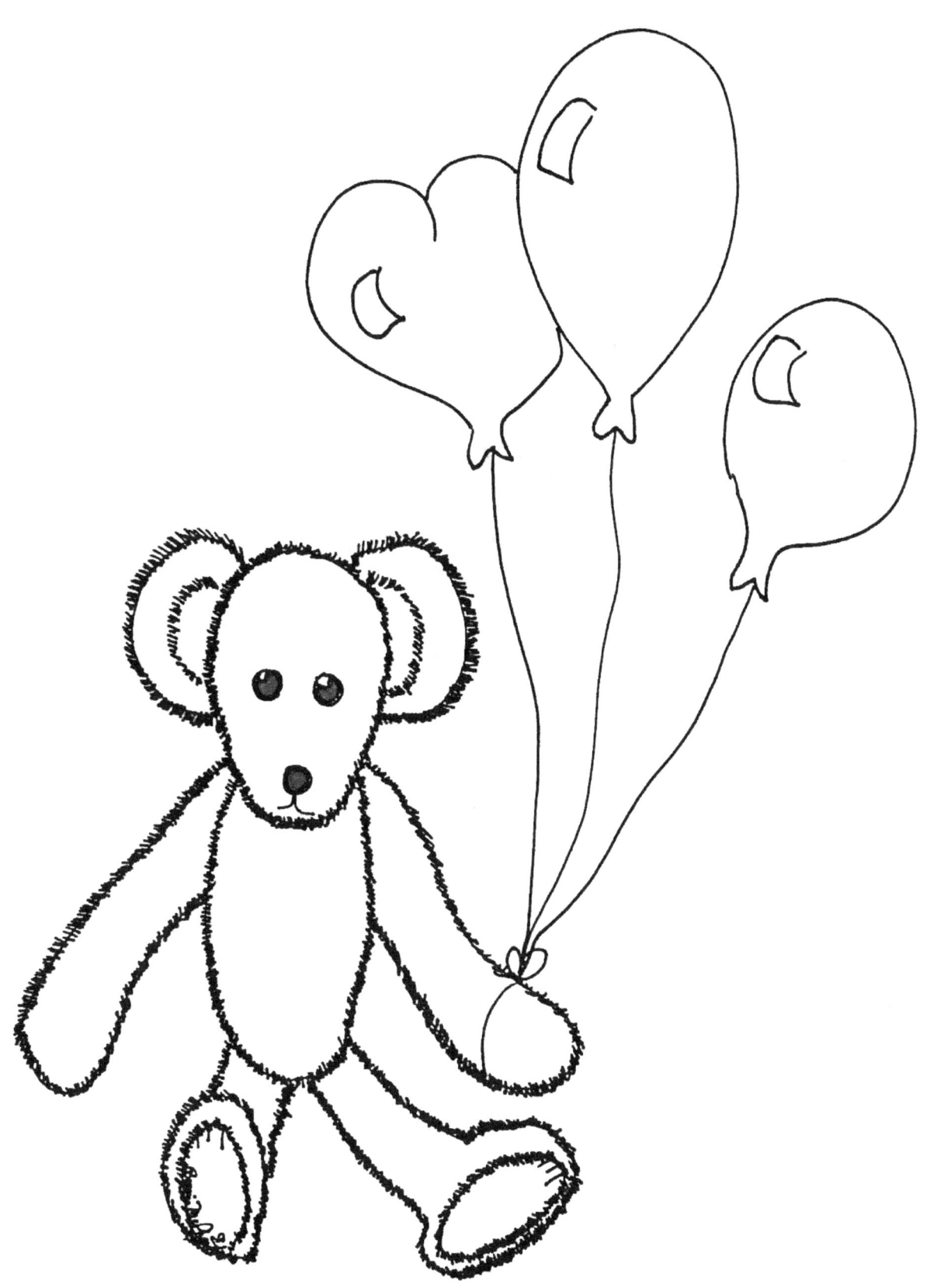

"Accept my heart and I'll build you a castle with love as its foundation."

Lifehacks.io

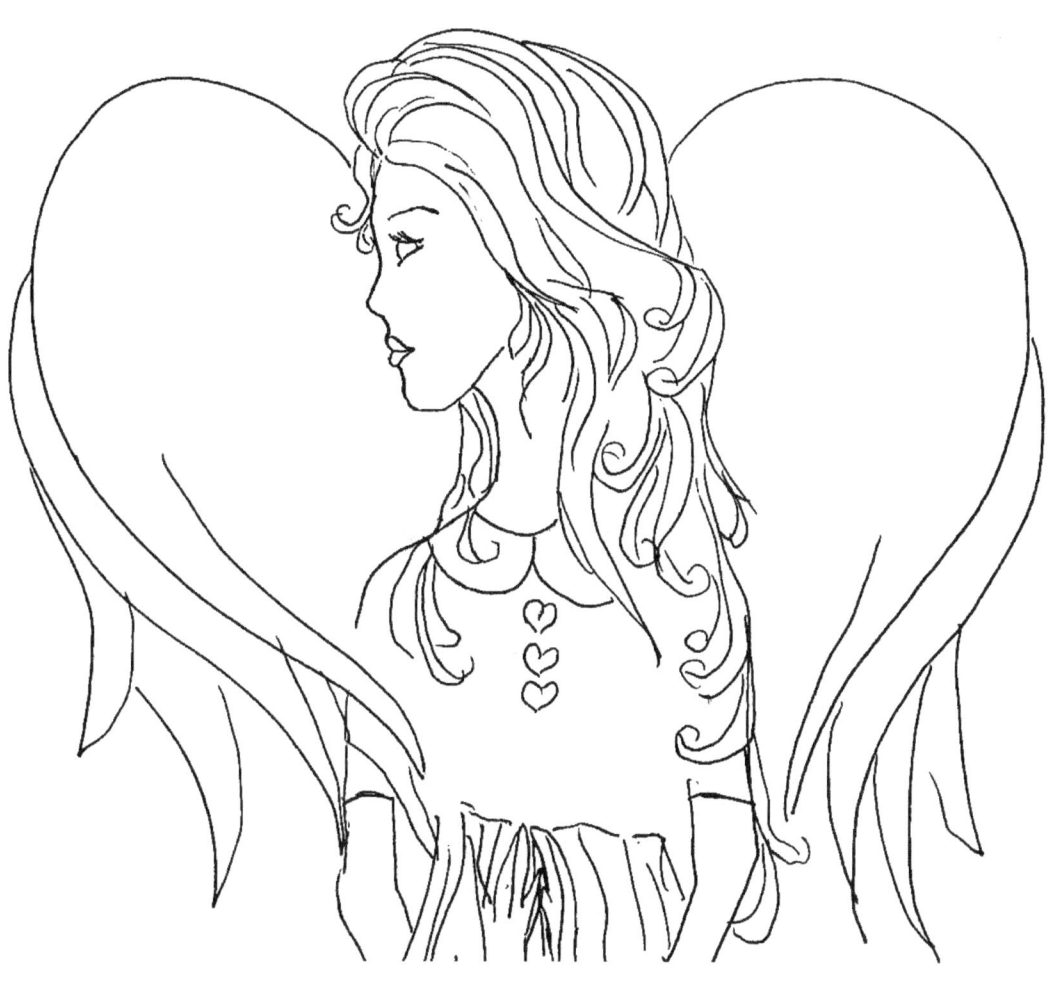

"Try to be a rainbow in someones cloud."

Maya Angelou

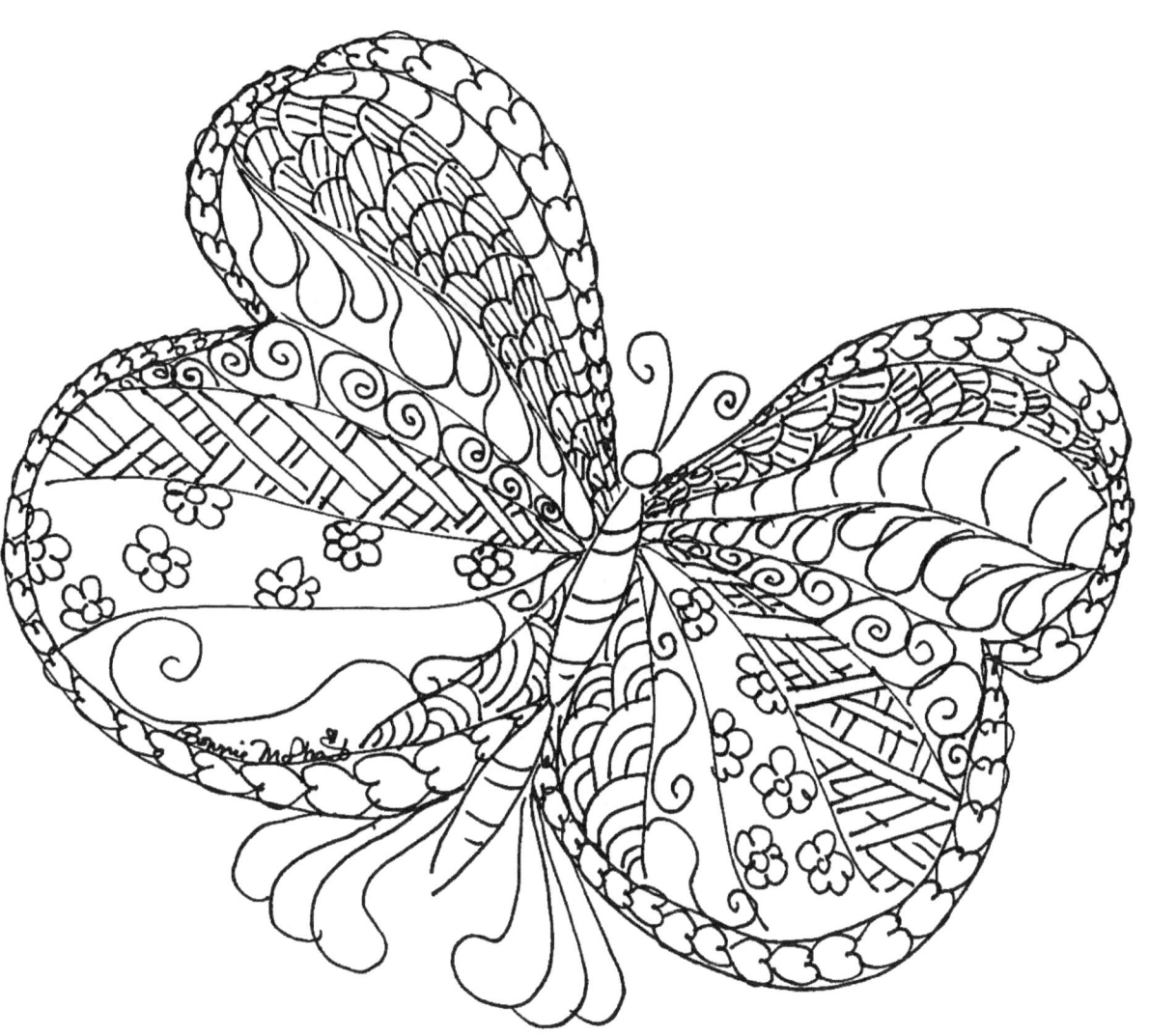

"Don't cry because it's over, smile because it happened."

Dr. Seuss

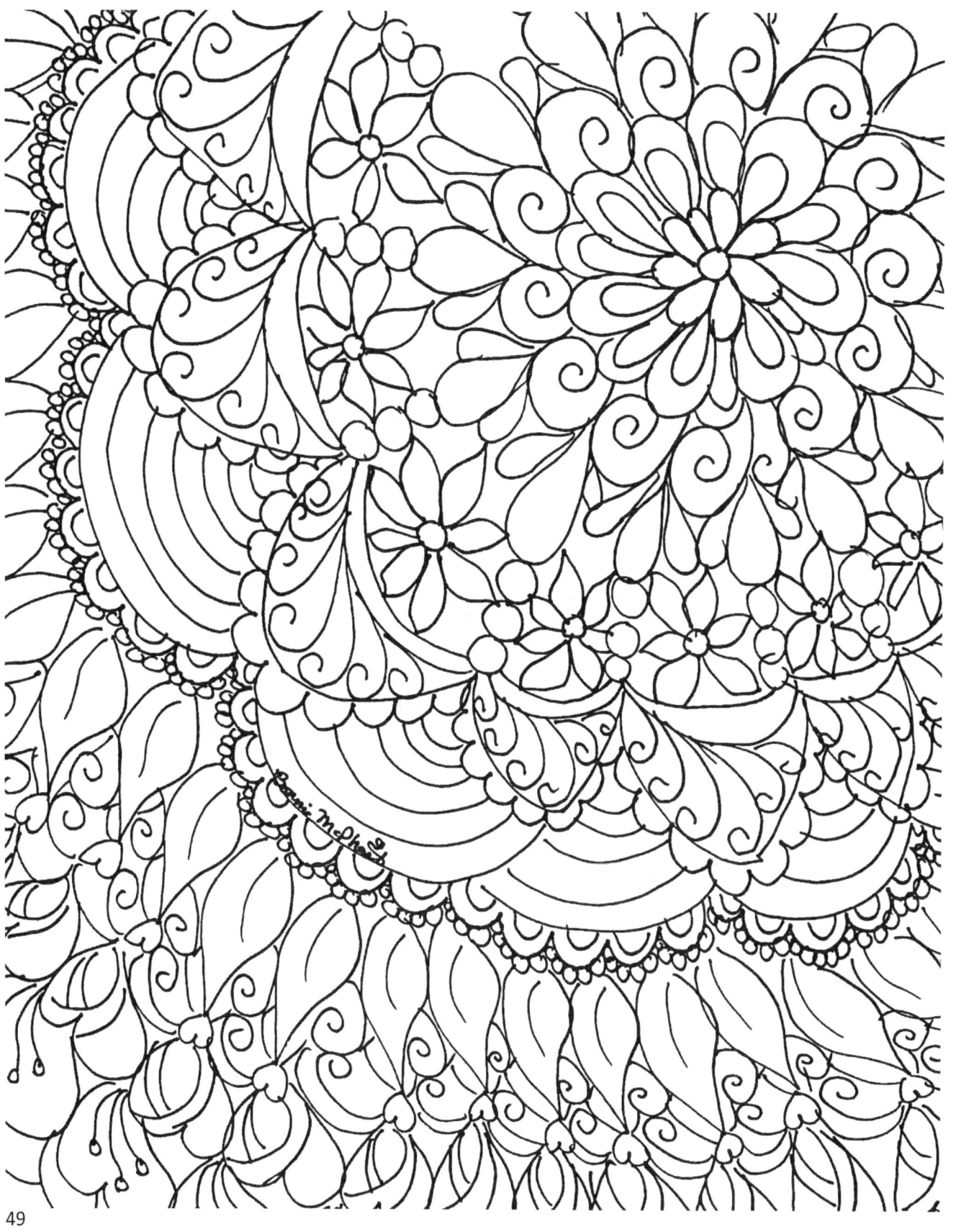

"You've gotta dance like there's nobody watching, love like you'll never be hurt,

Sing like there's nobody listening,

And live like it's heaven on earth."

William W. Purkey

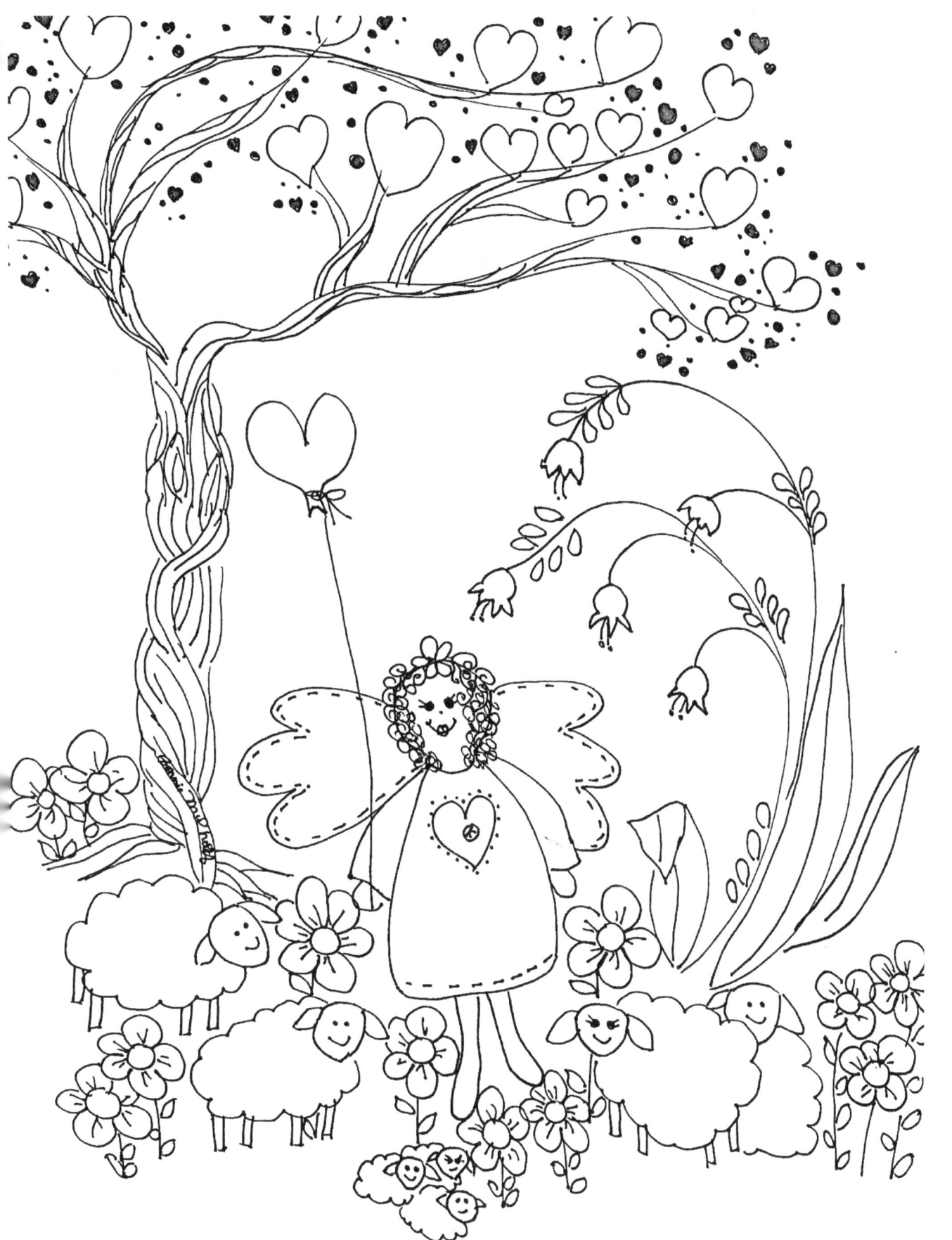

"You only live once, but if you do it right,

Once is enough."

Mae West

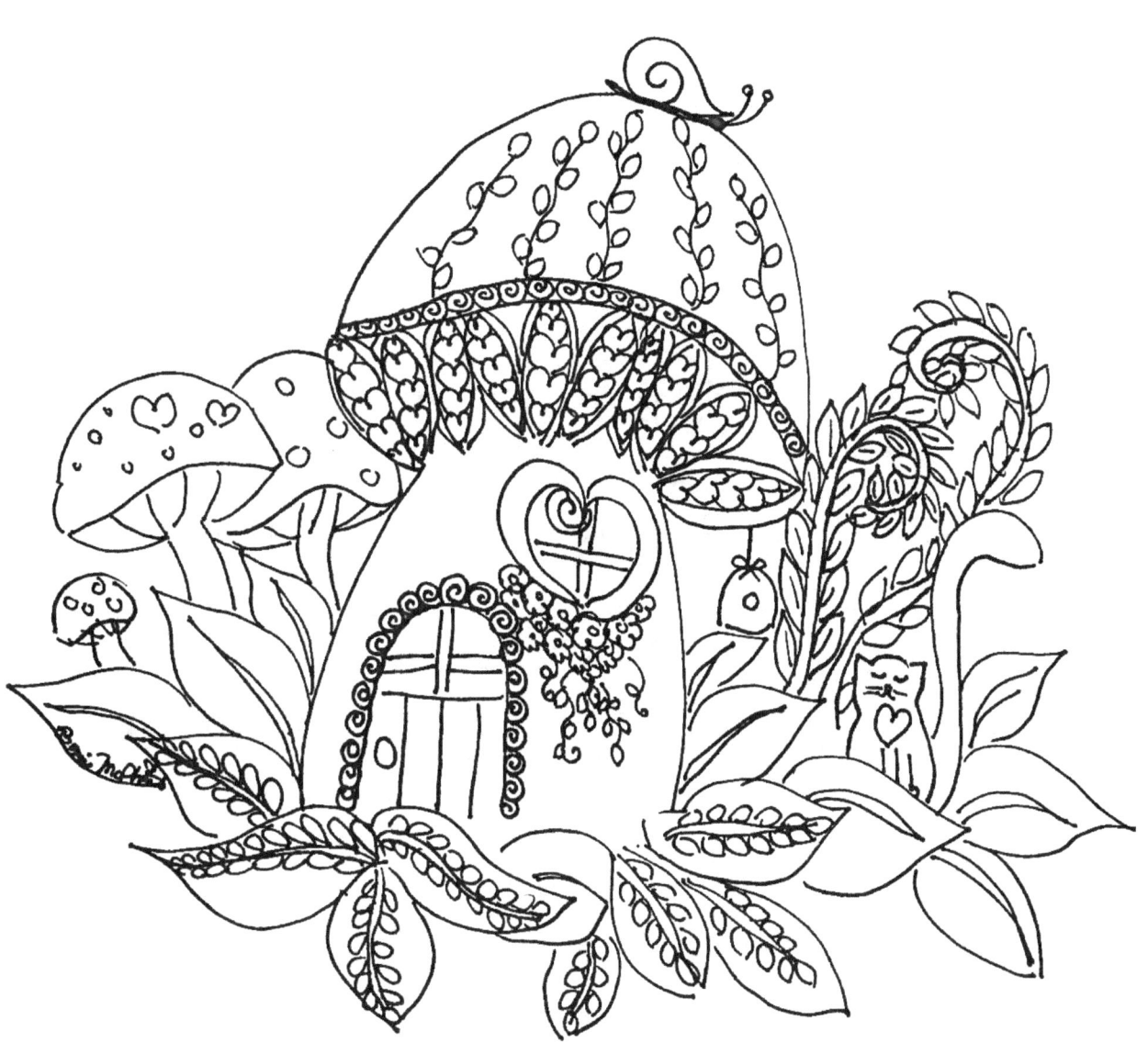

"Be the change

that you wish to see in the world."

Mahatma Gandhi

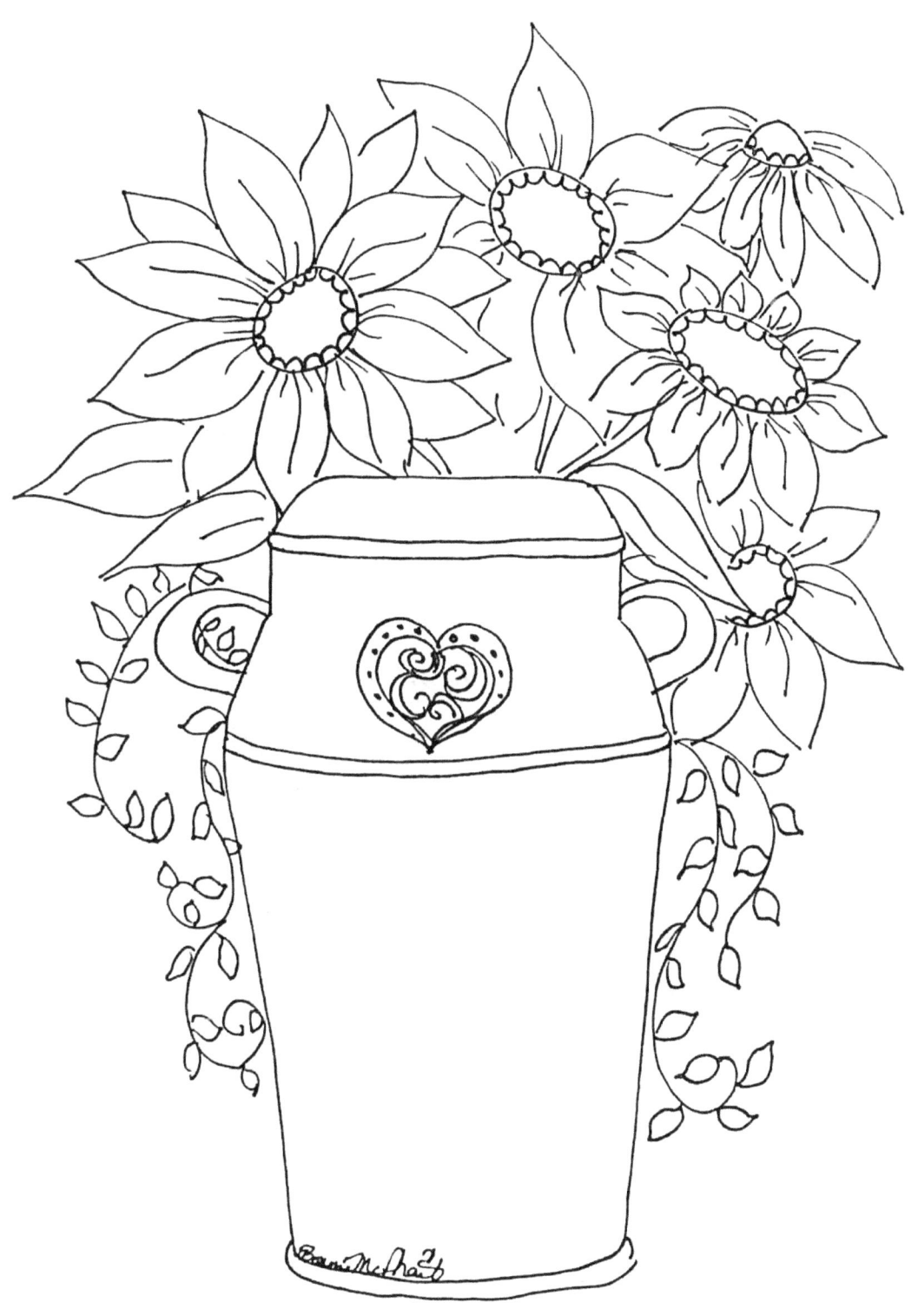

"Don't walk in front of me...

I may not follow.

Don't walk behind me...

I may not lead.

Walk beside me...

Just be my friend."

Albert Camus

Bonnie McPhail has graduated from the University of New York with a A.S.N in nursing, Rhema Bible Training College with certifications both in Pastoral Studies and Life Coaching, and from Oklahoma Wesleyan University with a B.S. in Organizational Management and Ethics.
She is an ordained Assembly of God minister. Her nursing background gives her special insight into the emotional and physical needs of people.

Her work has been published both nationally and internationally, and she is available for conferences and workshops.

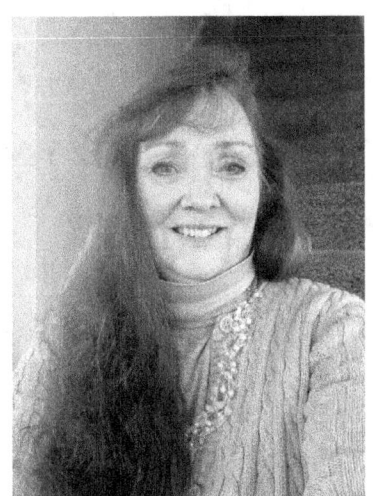

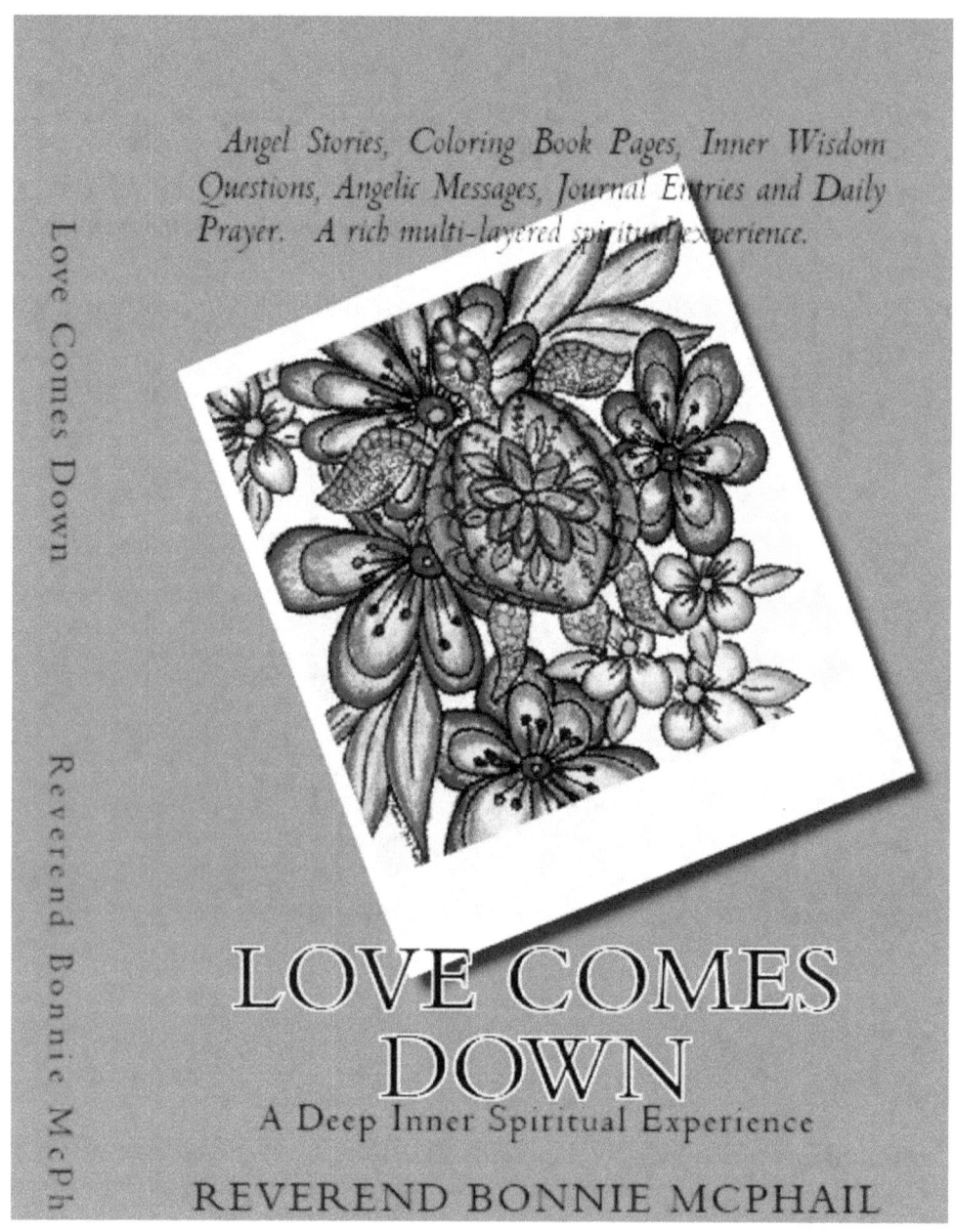

This is my personal favorite out of all hundred or more books the Lord has graced me to write. It is by far the best and most important work. This book combines personal inspirational life stories and actual encounters with angels, there are places for you to write your thoughts and prayers and a daily devotional. This book also contains over 60 pages of original artwork for you to color and make your own, even the headers at the top of each page are designed to be colored in. The pieces are integrated throughout the book with many at the end of the book that have a blank space to write your thoughts, dreams, ideas and prayers. A keepsake to go back and see what the Lord was doing in your life of your own thoughts idea, dreams, prayers, and I promise you the Lord will speak personally and directly to you as you spend time in the pages of this book. This book is designed not to just read but to truly be a rich, meaningful and powerful experience.